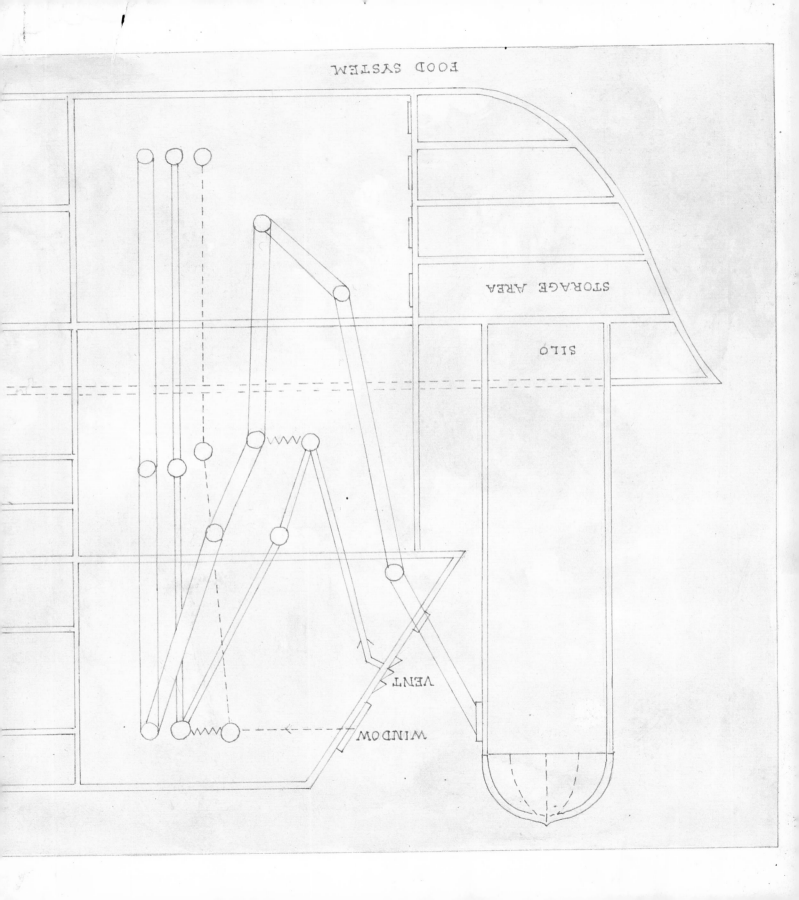

THE ARK

ANIMALS OF THE NORTH

ANIMALS OF THE WEST

NOAH AND
FAMILY

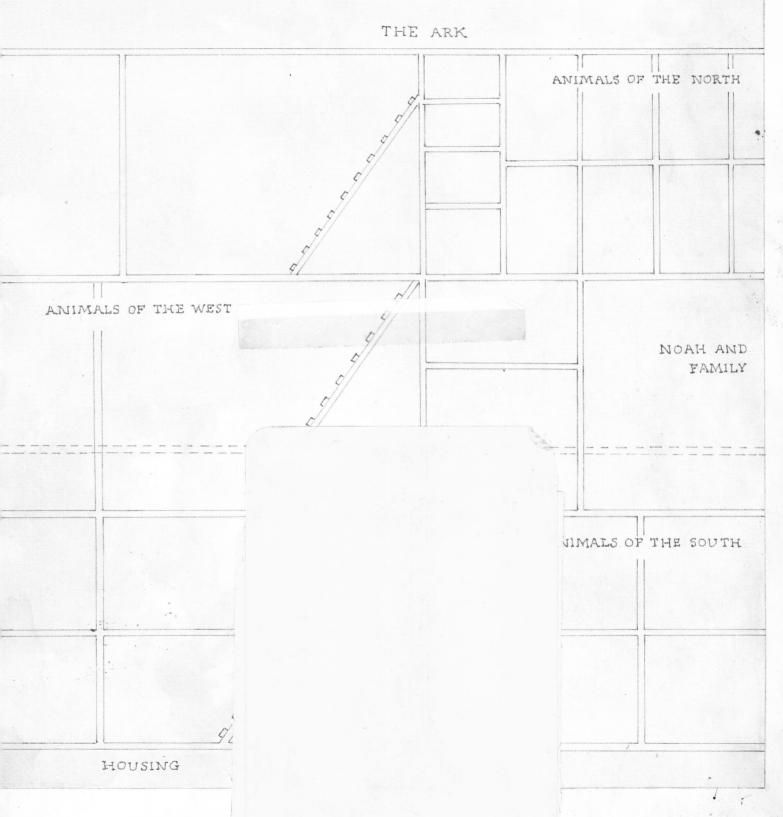

NIMALS OF THE SOUTH

HOUSING

NOAH'S ARK

ILLUSTRATED BY NONNY HOGROGIAN

ALFRED A. KNOPF, NEW YORK

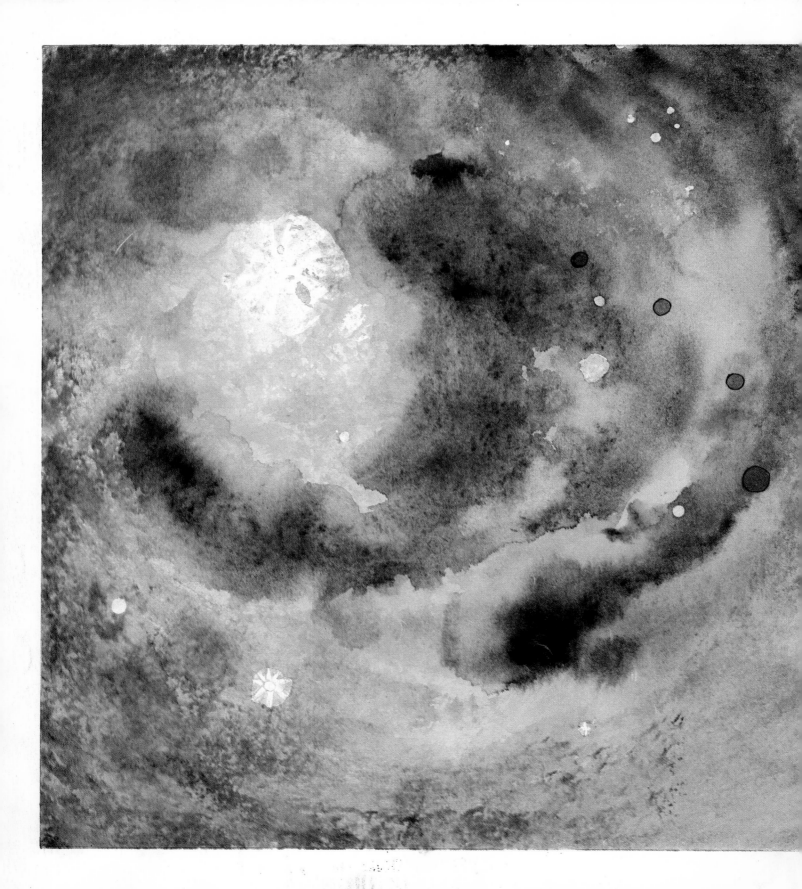

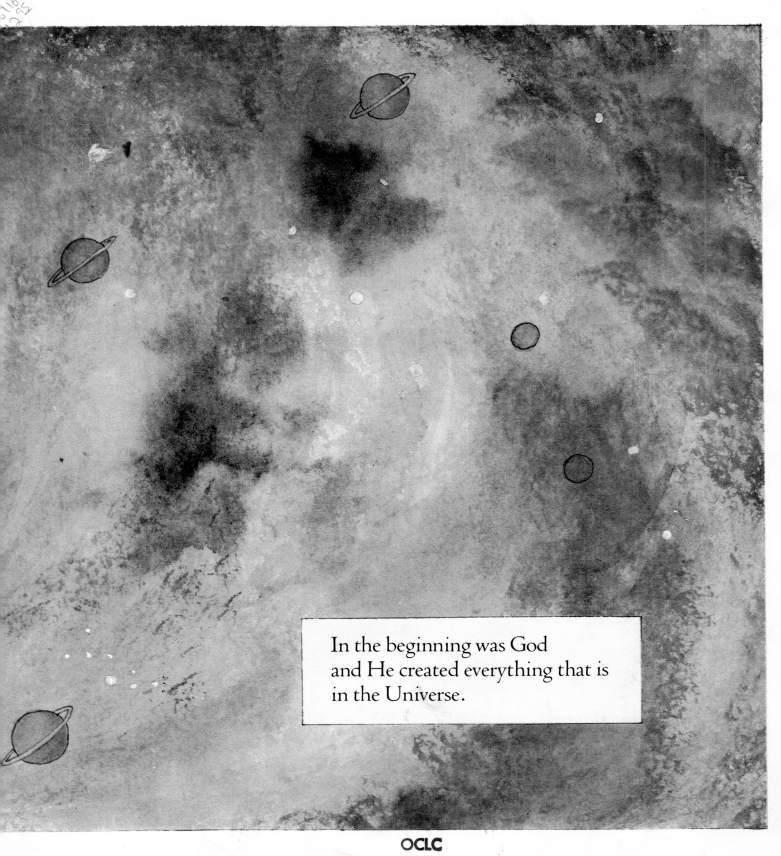

In the beginning was God
and He created everything that is
in the Universe.

And He created the Earth
and all that lives upon it
and in it,
the great whales of the seas,
and all the winged creatures of the air.

And He created Man,
male and female, to multiply
and to care for all that exists
on the Earth.
And Adam and Eve were the beginning
of the Generations of Man,

and Noah was the son of Lamech,
who was the son of Methuselah,
who was the son of Enoch,
who was the son of Jared,

who was the son of Mahalaleel,
who was the son of Cainan,
who was the son of Enos,
who was the son of Seth,
who was the third son of Adam and Eve.

And the human race began to multiply
upon the face of the Earth.

And many hundreds of years had passed
and God saw that wickedness
had filled the hearts of men
and it caused him great suffering.

And He looked at Noah
and only Noah found grace in the eyes of the Lord
and did all that God commanded him.
And God said to Noah
that He would send a flood
to destroy the wickedness on the Earth
and all that He had made
and He would begin again.
And God commanded Noah to make an Ark.

And Noah built the Ark as God commanded.
He built it 300 cubits long
and 50 cubits wide and 30 cubits high
and he sealed it with pitch.
God gave him the measure and placement
of the window and the door
and told him to build it in three stories
and Noah did as God commanded.

And God told Noah
to come into the Ark
with his sons and his wife
and his sons' wives
and all the other animals—
two by two—
a male and a female of every kind.

And in seven days the rains came
and the flood came upon the Earth
and Noah entered the Ark
with his sons and his wife
and the wives of his sons
and two of every kind of beast and bird
and every thing that creeps upon the Earth
with food for all
and seed with which to begin again.
The door was closed behind them.

And the rains came for forty days
and the Ark was lifted
upon the surface of the waters
and rose above the hills
until even the highest mountains were covered.
And all was destroyed that lived on the Earth
except Noah and all he cared for in the Ark.

And the flood was on the Earth
for one hundred and fifty days
and God looked on the Ark
and sent a wind over the Earth
and the waters receded.

And in the seventh month the Ark rested
upon the mountains of Ararat
and Noah sent forth a raven
who traveled to and fro
until he could find a place to rest.

And then Noah sent forth a dove as well
but the dove could find no resting place
and soon returned to the Ark.

And after seven days
Noah sent forth the dove once again
and in the evening the dove returned
with an olive leaf in her bill,
so Noah knew the waters had abated
but still he waited another seven days.

Noah sent forth the dove for the third time
but this time the dove did not return
and Noah knew the Earth was dry again
and the door of the Ark was opened.

And all of the animals went forth,
two of every kind,

and Noah went forth
and his sons and his wife
and the wives of his sons
and they took with them the seeds
that Noah had kept.

And God said in his heart
that no more would He curse the ground
for Man's sake.
While the Earth remains,
seedtime and harvest shall not cease.
And God told Noah that no more
would the waters become a flood.
And Noah tilled the soil
and with the seeds he had saved
he planted a vineyard.

THE BEGINNING

THIS IS A BORZOI BOOK PUBLISHED BY ALFRED A. KNOPF, INC.

Copyright © 1986 by Nonny H. Kherdian
All rights reserved under International and Pan-American Copyright
Conventions. Published in the United States by Alfred A. Knopf, Inc.,
New York, and simultaneously in Canada by Random House of
Canada Limited, Toronto. Distributed by Random House,
Inc., New York. Manufactured in the United States of America
1 3 5 7 9 0 8 6 4 2

Library of Congress Cataloging-in-Publication Data
Hogrogian, Nonny. Noah's ark. Summary: Retells the Old Testament
story of how Noah built an ark and saved one pair of every species
of animal on the earth when God sent the great flood.
1. Noah's ark—Juvenile literature. [1. Noah (Biblical figure) 2. Noah's ark.
3. Bible stories—O.T.] I. Title. BS658.H64 1986 222'.1109505 86-97
ISBN 0-394-88191-5   ISBN 0-394-98191-X (lib. bdg.)